FINDING HERMES' LETTER

A Fable for Our Daughters

ANNETTE MOSER-WELLMAN

Copyright © 2012 Annette Moser-Wellman
All rights reserved.
ISBN: 0615582370
ISBN-13: 9780615582375

This is my letter to the World
That never wrote to Me—
The simple News that Nature told—
With tender Majesty

Her Message is committed
To Hands I cannot see—
For love of Her—Sweet—countrymen—
Judge tenderly—of Me

- Emily Dickinson

To my daughters,
Constance Moser Wellman
and Georgia Moser Wellman

With whom all things are possible

FORWARD

There are few times in life when, as Rilke describes, "you are suddenly the catcher of a ball thrown by an eternal partner." I felt this "bridge-building of God" in my first book, *The Five Faces of Genius,* as well as in this short story, *Finding Hermes' Letter.* This is a tale about creativity through powers greater than ourselves—the "divine download."

I feel an urgency to record my best wisdom for my daughters and all daughters of the world. I've thought since a young age that I had a destiny to fulfill and in this writing hope to bring that purpose one step closer to fruition. The question consumes me still: what is more important than to express our unique, creative genius for the sake of the world? Perhaps our story's heroine, Barjinder can be a guide for us all.

Finding Hermes' Letter

My hope is that you feel this story is a ball thrown from God, and as you catch it you can begin to create for the sake of the world.

> Annette Moser-Wellman
> January 2012

JUST THIS SIDE OF THE LAND OF NOD

Dusty feet.

Barjinder felt awash in dust. The brown earth swirled around her feet, her body, everything in her simple house at the edge of the Punjab plain. As she stamped the mat at the entrance to the door, she looked down at her feet decorated in celebration the night before. "Why henna my feet when no one can see them for the dust?" she grumbled to herself. As the paneled door slammed behind her, she promised herself a future in which the air was clear and life was fully colored.

FINDING HERMES' LETTER

In the tilted afternoon light, she noticed her father at the table making naan for the evening meal. Barjinder's stomach tightened in frustration as she watched the familiar kneading movements. These last months, her father's habits bothered her more and more. Everything did. Routine made her feel she was waiting for life to happen. As she greeted him, she struggled to be kind.

"Father, must you stoop so when you knead the bread? Tonight you will complain of your back aching."

"Thank you, Daughter," he replied, accepting her words and straightening his shoulders against the dough.

She walked quickly to her room and closed the door. She draped her scarf behind the door and slumped at the desk chair. Ever since her mother had died, Barjinder and her father shared the family responsibilities. His baking supported them, and when she was not in school, she earned money taking care of chores for others in the small village. Her father loved her faithfully, but the time to begin her own life was fast approaching. Almost sixteen now, she longed to travel away from the village—to start a new life in the city. She wanted to stop waiting. She wanted to spend her life doing things that mattered. She imagined that work should mean more than putting food on the table.

Barjinder dropped her head to her desk. Her memory pulsed with a tale her mother told in the quiet moments of their short time together.

"Hermes, the great messenger, has a letter for each person that explains her purpose in life. This is a great letter because it will help you design your future. But every person must venture to find it for herself. Hermes will find you on the journey and deliver your letter—a message just for you."

Barjinder was not sure that she had remembered her mother's story clearly, but the fragment in her mind was enough to prompt her to ask her father about it once again. Her restlessness about her future couldn't wait. That night at dinner, she chanced mentioning what she knew would be painful. Her mother's death had shut away his memories. "Father, tell me about Hermes' Letter," she said.

Her father didn't raise his eyes from his meal. Barjinder was surprised when he began to speak deliberately, as if he had been preparing his answer to her question for months. "Each person may search for Hermes' Letter when she is ready. This letter will tell you of your greatest passions and purpose in life. But the journey to find it is dangerous. It carries a high price. I began the journey into the Land of Nod but was forced to turn back." He looked directly at Barjinder. "Yet, I have had a good life without knowing the contents of that letter. I think you would agree."

Barjinder studied his gentle eyes and answered softly, "Yes, Father. You've had a good life." She wanted to ask more, to say more, but the feeling of her father's burden was palpable, so she rose instead and quietly lifted their dishes from the table.

That night her bones fought the thin mattress beneath her. She dreamed of insects with wide protrusions boring into the flesh of her thighs. When she tried to pull the pincers out, she couldn't repair the damage they had done. When she awoke with a start, she calmed herself by thinking hard about Hermes' Letter and the path to get to the Land of Nod. Even in her half-asleep state, she knew what she would do: visit the woman-guide who lived near the base of the mountain ridge.

The next day after work, Barjinder walked the distance to Durga's house. She learned of the wise one from the people of the village. Although they considered her wild, villagers spoke of Durga with a soft reverence. Barjinder could see Durga in the back garden, tending what looked like a dusty patch of weeds. As Barjinder approached, Durga noticed her visitor's shadow. With gaze held down, she curtly directed Barjinder away.

"I have nothing here for you. Leave me be," she said.

"But Durga, some say you are wise, and I need your help," Barjinder replied calmly.

"Can't you see I'm busy? I can't be bothered." Hunkered down in the brown dust, Durga clipped a pod from a tangled vine with her thick, ridged thumbnail.

Barjinder crouched next to her and began helping Durga pluck the pods off the dried stems.

"I want to talk about Hermes' Letter," Barjinder began.

Durga turned her head and glared at Barjinder. One eye was blue and the other a luminous milky red. Barjinder was caught off guard. She quickly looked away with fear. It was a few moments before she could look up and return to the woman's gaze. When Durga was satisfied with the girl's courage, she slowly righted her pear-shaped body, collected her basket of pods, and said, "Come with me."

Barjinder followed her through the back door of her home and entered a high-ceiling room. The familiar layer of dust covered everything from the spare furniture to the leftover breakfast dishes on the table. The room seemed suspended in time, as if no one had lived there long enough to disrupt the powdery earth. Durga turned and faced Barjinder;

she did not invite her to sit. Barjinder wrestled with her tongue and tried to make words come out.

Hung from the high ceiling were cages filled with different types of birds. Pheasants shuffled through shreds of paper. Blue and pink cockatiels chirped. A large parrot cackled and scraped from the corner cage. Durga walked from cage to cage. She began speaking in an impatient tone.

"The search for Hermes' Letter is only for those who have great courage. Perhaps that's you. Perhaps it isn't. The search begins this side of the Land of Nod—the path just beyond the high hill. Be prepared for a journey of many days or a few days. Be prepared to leave your life behind. And be prepared to never have it back again.

"If you think you have this courage, go home. Tell your family that you are going to leave to find your life's purpose. If you have the true desire, you will come to see me tomorrow before the sun has risen full off the horizon. If you develop an infection of your initiative, do not come to me again. Now go."

Finding Hermes' Letter

As Durga led her back out the door into the bright sun, Barjinder squinted. She wanted to ask more questions, yet she remained unable to speak. As Durga motioned for her to go, Barjinder looked at her unflinchingly.

Walking home, Barjinder knew what she wanted to do. She knew she must leave. Yet she also knew she would not be able to tell her father. Her leaving would break his already lonely heart.

That evening Barjinder and her father prepared dinner in silence. She found herself moving close to him to take in his comforting smell before she went to her room. There she began to write a note. "Dear Father, As you once did, I go to search for Hermes' Letter. I want to do more with my life than struggle for money. I know you love me as I love you. I will miss you, but expect me home soon with letter in hand. Your daughter, Barjinder."

She took her leather pack and stuffed it with her warmest sweater, overcoat, and sturdy shoes. That night she watched the moon rise and slept with one eye toward the eastern horizon.

When she rose at dawn, she quietly dressed and slipped into the dark to pack food from the kitchen. There she was startled to find the silhouette of her father. He stood behind the table preparing parcels of food. He said, "I want you to have what you need for your journey." She realized her father had sensed her plans. She ran to him. "Oh, Father. I will be careful. I will return with my letter."

"Yes, Daughter. Your fate has arrived. The longer you wait to begin the search, the greater the chance you'll never begin. Move forward." Together they finished packing her bag, and with the sun now rising, she knew she had to hurry.

He handed Barjinder a small piece of folded paper, worn on the edges. "This map was given to me to help me find my way to Hermes' Letter. I'm not certain if it is a good map, or even if it will lead you to your letter. But it is all I have and I wish you to have it. Return to me, Daughter." Barjinder pressed the map into the pocket of her pants, turned toward the sun, and ran the distance to Durga's.

Finding Hermes' Letter

Barjinder knocked on the back door. The sun was nearly off the horizon. She banged the door. Her waiting was mixed with a strange hope. "If Durga doesn't come, then the decision to stay will have been made for me." She banged again, more insistently. "Hello?!"

When no one answered, Barjinder reached down and twisted the handle of the door and opened it. The morning light streamed through the bars of the birdcages. They were empty, yet their noises were everywhere. She turned, and something tangled at the back of her hair. She thwacked her neck with her hand, bent down, and wrenched free of what felt like a wing. With her heart racing, she stood up and looked straight into a small red light. "Durga!"

"So you've come."

Durga shooed a bird off of a chair at the dusty table and lowered her heaviness into it. Barjinder watched Durga's red eye seem to trail light as it moved. "The Land of Nod begins with a boot-built path circling up the edge of the vista. You'll notice the entrance by two twisted bushes of bramble thorns. You must look for food wherever you can along the journey. Eat as much as you can so you will not lose your strength. Hermes' Letter comes to different people in different ways, so I cannot tell you how it will come or even if you will find yours. But I see you do not fear risk and dare. That is good. I've always said, 'Only crazy people walk close to the safety of walls.'"

"Sir Topas," she called with authority. Presently, a colorful parrot shuffled across the room and leaped onto the table. She perched the bird on her arm. The parrot was old, with flecks of gray in his feathers and chips on the side of his curved beak.

"This parrot will be your constant companion. Carry him with you at all times. His name is Sir Topas. He can only mirror what you say. You may find him a help…or not. I only ask that, at the end of your journey, you return Sir Topas to me."

Barjinder mustered, "Durga, how will I know the way?"

"You won't," she said simply. "That is what makes it a journey."

Durga picked up Barjinder's pack, set Sir Topas on Barjinder's shoulder, and directed the two out through the open door.

THE TINKER'S CABIN

Barjinder circled around the back of Durga's dry garden. She knew the high hill of which Durga had spoken. Barjinder had lifted her eyes from the plains to that vista throughout her girlhood. She had never stopped wondering what lay beyond. Now she would find out.

She felt an urgency to move quickly. Once she recognized the gate of twisted thorns ahead, she began running. Sir Topas flapped and clung tightly to the shoulder straps of her pack. As she passed through the gate, a circular pattern in the dust caught her eye. She stopped, reached down, and uncovered a slender coiled rope woven from long grass. Instinctively Barjinder knew to keep it. She tied the cord to the top of her pack.

Finding Hermes' Letter

She could see the trail winding up the foothill. It began as dust, deepened to orange earth, then traced back and forth across the bare mountain. With intention, she headed up. With each switchback, she leaned forward for balance. Her breathing grew heavier as the cluster of low buildings in the prairie below began to shrink. She felt surprising relief as she watched the town shrink in her view.

The higher Barjinder climbed, the more her mind filled with questions. "Perhaps I was too hasty in leaving my father. Why should I find my letter, when Father never found his? Why didn't I ask Durga what supplies were needed?" And she resented having to bring Sir Topas. With each new incline, he awkwardly adjusted his claws and shifted his weight. His feathers scratched against Barjinder's cheek with a peculiar and unpleasant scent. Thankfully, she thought, he was proving quiet.

As she reached the crest of the hill, she looked back and was rewarded with a view unlike anything she had ever seen. The tiny town spread before her, as did the dry hills that lay beyond. She surveyed how high she had climbed and how small the dusty valley was. Her questions fell away, and she knew she had to continue the journey. It was her chance to find a new future.

Barjinder turned to look ahead. She could see the Land of Nod was going to be much different than what she'd known before. Fields of green grasses, rolling hills, and white mountains scaled the distance. She allowed herself a gulp of water from her gourd and walked forward toward the green.

Barjinder had dreamed about Hermes' Letter. She learned the name *Hermes* from the ancients who had inhabited the land of her people. Her home was at the edge of the Punjab, the land of five rivers: the Beas, Sutlej, Ravi, Chenab, and Jhelum. She knew the Greeks called this *Pentopotamia*—the place where the rivers meet from the greatest mountain range. Hermes was the messenger of a powerful Greek god who lived within these mountains.

After a time, she decided to pull out the map her father had given her. She relieved herself of Sir Topas and sat down on the side of the path. He seemed to be grateful to be on the ground and wandered away into some long grasses. Barjinder could hear him tearing at the stalks with his powerful beak. "He seems ravenous," she thought. "How am I going to keep him satisfied?"

She carefully unfolded the map and began studying it. In her father's handwriting she read the title, "The Land of Nod." She recognized her hike up the hill and noticed a winding path, but she saw no clear destination. The only marker labeled on the path was "Tinker's Cabin."

From where she had come, the distance to the Tinker's Cabin did not seem a far hike. Perhaps she could find shelter there for the night. She was beginning to get hungry but wanted to save her supplies. Grabbing her satchel, she went to collect Sir Topas. Clearly he wasn't finished eating. He was clasping a clump of grass tightly, and when she went to tug him away, she fell backward with the force. "Not just smelly, but stubborn too," she said. She had to wait a while, until she could catch him between bites, then swiftly placed him back onto the saddle of her shoulder. She headed out.

In the distance she saw smoke trailing from a scraggly grove of trees. "Surely this is the Tinker's Cabin," she thought. The trail soon revealed a low, mossy-roof structure. She heard rumbling from Sir Topas. A muffled growl emanated from his gullet, and by the time she reached the door, the parrot was cackling loudly as if to announce their coming. "What's wrong with him?" she thought.

She knocked on the front door. A diminutive man with the face of a young boy greeted her. "Hello, Barjinder! Welcome!"

"How do you know my name?" she asked, taken aback.

"I've been expecting you. Please do come in." As she walked into the warm room, she noticed that the boyish face of her host was, surprisingly, connected to the frame of a short old man. He shuffled across the floor as if to protect his body from some familiar pain.

Sir Topas blurted out, "How do you know my name? How do you know my name?" Barjinder started and stared at the parrot. "Now, he speaks," she thought.

"Sir Topas. Stop. You are being rude," Barjinder shushed him.

"No harm," replied the Tinker. "I'm sure we can satisfy the old bird." Barjinder blushed when he mentioned age. Didn't the Tinker realize he was half old himself?

He found a shallow bowl and filled it with seeds from one of the many jars that lined the cabin walls. He placed it on the floor in front of Sir Topas, who proceeded to feed himself with utter concentration.

"And you're hungry as well," the Tinker said to Barjinder. "Let's prepare dinner together."

The little man began pulling jars from the wall and setting them on the table in the center of the room. "Swallowwort, yes. Crushed mango twig, yes. Dried lotus leaf and lentil seed, of course."

As the table filled with jars, he explained, "Folks call me the Tinker because I experiment with everything—especially herbs. None of these items alone may appeal to you, but when you mix things together and try them, you'll be surprised how they can please."

Barjinder wasn't exactly sure what the Tinker meant, but it was nice to have someone take on the task of offering direction after a long day of finding her own way. There was a certain ease and comfort in his presence. He was an odd mixture of the hope of youth and the wisdom of age. She surprised herself by saying aloud, "I am in search of Hermes' Letter."

"Yes. I'm told my cabin is the first stop on the way through the Land of Nod. I greet many who are looking to find their letter of purpose."

"So, I am in the Land of Nod now?"

"Yes."

"How can I tell?"

"In the Land of Nod, the space between heaven and earth is thin. The laws of nature are mutable, and we see things as they might be."

He handed Barjinder a deep, broad mug and invited her to dip her spoon in the large jars arranged on the table. As she added ingredients, she followed the Tinker's lead in grinding the items in her cup with the back of her large spoon. When she had turned everything into a fine powder, the Tinker pulled from the fire a kettle filled with hot liquid and poured it into her cup. The steam from the mug hovered and the Tinker motioned for her to sip with her spoon.

She began drinking this soup. More comfortable now, she had started to ask him how he knew her name when she saw something out of the corner of her eye—an image—in the cloud of steam. Barjinder shook her head. Was she now imagining things, tired from the journey? She returned her attention to the soup. But as Barjinder looked away, she saw again a figure of a woman with a flowing skirt wrapping around her legs.

"Do you see that?" Barjinder earnestly asked the Tinker as she pointed to her mug.

He sipped calmly and said, "Drink your soup," but he smiled.

Barjinder stared at the steam but saw nothing. Exhausted, she tried to relax.

"So, you know a lot about the Land of Nod?" Barjinder began asking, but as she looked up at him, the woman appeared again, just below her line of sight. The woman's face had no features; it was only full of light.

"There it is again!" Barjinder exclaimed, confidently this time.

The Tinker looked at her and said, "Every experiment will yield its own results. Every mixture creates something new."

Hungry, Barjinder continued drinking her soup, and with every sip she felt herself filling up as if she were eating a glorious meal. The simple powder gave her a rush of satisfaction. Soon the need to sleep forced her to ask for a place to spread out her blanket. The Tinker directed her to a storage room, and she gratefully lay down for the night.

She awoke to the screech of Sir Topas' voice, "Only crazy people walk close to walls. Crazy people walk close to walls." She vowed to speak as little as possible on this trip so she wouldn't go crazy from his odd chorus of repeated words.

Eager to face the day, Barjinder gathered her things and found the Tinker already at the center table. "Good morning!" he offered with his impish smile. "Hungry for breakfast?"

"Why, no," she said, surprised. "I'm not hungry. In fact, I'm quite full from last night."

"Yes! Another of my inventions," he responded happily. "The liquid I used last night in your soup stores high levels of energy within your body. The energy will last you for many days!" He seemed quite pleased with himself, and she thought he would jump up and down with glee if his body had been young enough.

He went on. "Traveling through the Land of Nod is not an easy journey. In fact, I'm told it can be quite dangerous. Expect trials ahead. As I have always been the first stop, I'm not exactly sure what the future might hold."

"What more can you tell me?" Barjinder asked eagerly.

"I do know that the journey ends at the place called Hermes' Wing. There you will be given the letter that you so long for."

New doubts about her ability to make it through the journey flooded her mind as he spoke. She steeled herself and tried to think only of herself at Hermes' Wing.

Reading her keenly, the Tinker offered, "If you are unsure of your resolve, turning back now would be a good idea." He reasoned, "The deeper you journey in the Land of Nod, the harder it is to get back. That is, if you can get back at all."

Barjinder was silent.

The Tinker's weak arms reached into his jacket pockets, and he pulled out two small leather pouches, each tightly bound with a cord at the top. "Because I have not influenced you to turn aside, you may need these for your journey." The edges of his grin were boyishly crooked as he added, "They are special inventions. One will heal and the other will make you sick. I would like to tell you which is which, but it's not for me to say."

Barjinder became angry. She expected the Tinker to help her find Hermes' Letter, not confuse her. The thought that he might not be trusted slid into her mind. She had intended to show him her father's map and ask for more direction. Now, she felt the need to move on, and quickly.

She put the pouches in her pack and turned to leave. As she approached the door, she swung around and asked, "One last thing. How did you know my name?"

"Oh. Sir Topas told me," he said, still smiling mischievously.

"How could Sir...Sir Topas!" She had almost left without him. Barjinder ran to find him in the storage room where she had slept. He had used his beak as a knife to slice a seed bag and was feeding mightily on what was spilling onto the floor. He was so bloated he could scarcely move. His soft feathers protruded from his underbelly.

"I must remember not to let him overeat!" she thought. Barjinder transferred him to her shoulder. He was even heavier than before. As she bid the Tinker good-bye, Sir Topas belched so loudly Barjinder had to offer apologies and thanks at the same time.

THE BUTTERFLY FIELD

The way of the trail seemed clear as it wound beyond the Tinker's Cabin. A brown saddle in the middle, the trail had plush moss on either side. The path was flat and the smell of the forest ahead brought thoughts of freedom and feelings of delight. Barjinder loved being outside, like a scout exploring the future. Tall trees with high canopy shaded the trail. She fell into an easy rhythm of walking, her mind drifting to thoughts of the Tinker. "How could he have known my name? And how could he claim Sir Topas told him? As if Sir Topas was capable of intelligent conversation!"

As she walked along with her thoughts, she forgot the weight on her shoulder and even her search for Hermes' Letter. Her mind drifted to her memories as a child. She remembered how she had found a dead mouse in the grain room of her father's bakery. Afraid, she called for him to come, and he cleaned up the mouse with a broom and dustpan. After the work was done, and the dustpan hung in the workshop, the very sight of it forever filled her with fear, as if the mouse still lay in the dustpan. It was a natural mistake for a child's mind, she realized, but she considered how that fantasy had piloted her mind toward ill. She wondered if her imagination could pilot her now toward the good.

Sir Topas chortled and drew Barjinder's thoughts back to the trail. "Smelly and stubborn." she thought. A warmth drifted from the wind ahead. The trail grew shallow and spilled out into a meadow of golden wheat. The sun had dried the long grasses, and the clearing was broad and wide. The great expanse signaled to Barjinder that it was time to rest. She took off her pack, released Sir Topas into the grass, and fell on her back.

She watched Sir Topas groom himself in the bright sunshine. He may be fat, she thought, but he could be seen as quite lovely, really—a palette of intense color. He preened behind his wings with his neck twisted full around. When he was done caring for himself, he nestled himself there and slept.

Barjinder took off her boots and stockings. She noticed the henna fading from her feet. Memories of the night of the village festival came rushing in. She felt growing remorse, thinking of dear friends she had left behind. There had been a boy there, someone whose family might mean a match for her. Yet, she wanted something more right now. She needed this letter. And she remembered her father and his charge that she must return to him. These thoughts powered her legs to stand up and take up her pack, and urged her to discover what lay ahead on the next section of trail.

Yet from this distance, she couldn't see through the meadow to where the trail began again. She hiked the diameter of the field looking for an exit. She searched to the left for a time and then retraced the circle back to the right. Barjinder feared she would have to walk the entire circle of the field to reclaim the trail. The afternoon sun was waning, and she wondered if she was lost.

Then she saw Sir Topas in the center of the field, flapping his wings and hopping in circles. A hum radiated from the forest glen and grew louder. Barjinder began to worry as she heard new screams from Sir Topas. From over the treetops appeared a swath of yellow against the blue sky. The vibrant yellow cloud rose, dipped in waves, and began to rush toward her. In fear she ran, believing it to be bees ready to attack. But as she turned her head to look, the swarm raced around her face and she saw butterflies all around, blowing their airy wings by her face and sending her hair flying behind her.

The fluttering swarm ascended from behind Barjinder, crested, and broke in two. The two groups formed a double-helix shape that spun in front of her, like a moving painting. The parts then peeled apart and spread to form a living blanket of yellow over the field. The butterflies shifted to form a checkerboard pattern and then folded back and rolled to their underside.

Barjinder was mesmerized by the show. A calm descended on the meadow, and she was amazed that so much motion produced such a quiet hum. The butterflies moved in almost mathematical patterns. She noticed the yellow mounds of wings continued to come back to one particular design before they pulsed to a new one. As Barjinder watched closely, the shape of a wing would appear over and over. Then she realized, the butterflies were signaling the direction to Hermes' Wing.

As if on cue, the mesmerizing peace woven by the butterflies was broken by Sir Topas's squawking, which had reached fever pitch. The swarm of butterflies began pushing against his tail feathers, trying to coax him to fly. It was hard to tell if he was afraid or angry, but he began flapping frantically. He raised himself off the ground with wings extended. He sailed such a good distance that Barjinder was shocked he could be airborne that long. She rushed to him.

"Great work, Sir Topas! You flew!" she said with proud excitement.

"Why certainly. I am a bird, you know," he replied.

Barjinder gasped, "Did you just talk to me?"

"Did you just talk to me?" he mimicked. "Of course I did." He continued with unexpected sass, "Did you think I could stay quiet with a swarm of butterflies attempting to accost me?"

Barjinder's shock at Sir Topas's words was surpassed only by her interest in where the butterflies were going. She needed direction to get out of the meadow.

"Let's go!" Barjinder cried, and Sir Topas flew to her shoulder. They watched the butterflies cluster at the edge of the meadow. They fluttered in swirls toward the trees, directing the pilgrim and her bird to their exit.

"Now, no running!" Sir Topas croaked. "When you bounce up and down, it gives me a headache!"

Barjinder wasn't sure she should believe her ears.

THE GREAT CREVASSE

For what seemed like days, Barjinder and Sir Topas traveled. But the journey seemed much less lonely now. Sir Topas liked to talk. He proved to be interested in many subjects—some Barjinder liked and others she didn't. Sir Topas was an expert in gastronomy and waxed on about foods of many cultures. Barjinder often asked him to stop because his descriptions of braised lamb with port wine reduction and other delicacies reminded her how very hungry they were becoming. She tried to inquire about Hermes' Letter, but after many questions, Sir Topas didn't seem to know anything about the search. Yet he continued to provide entertaining conversation, and Barjinder found the load of walking with him considerably lighter.

Finding Hermes' Letter

"Tell me about your life in the village," Sir Topas inquired. As Barjinder walked, she talked freely about her days with her father, and she even spoke of her mother. She found herself sharing things with Sir Topas she hadn't said aloud to anyone. "She would sit near me as I drew my letters. When I closed my eyes, she would kiss them as if she were blessing me. People tell me she had many gifts and talents."

"A person who shares my character, I see," Sir Topas said. "And your mother passed her gifts to you?"

"I don't know if I can say that. My mother was an artist of sorts. They say she drew the henna. She told me stories of the city to the south with all of its people, its colors, and her dreams to travel there."

"Oh yes, the variety of food in the city to the south!" Sir Topas went on. "A veritable feast. Their curries are very fine. I especially enjoy those."

As Sir Topas dreamed aloud of food, Barjinder worried about finding enough. She recalled Durga's warning that they would need much sustenance. Both were beginning to become hungry as the effects of the Tinker's concoction faded. From her pack, Barjinder pulled out some of the parcels her father had prepared for her. She began eating the dried meat and fruit. Sir Topas complained about the limited fare. "I am satisfied by neither the quality nor the quantity" became a familiar refrain.

Barjinder continued to study her father's map, trying to glean any last wisdom that the worn drawing might hold. She penciled in the days' distance from the thorny gate to the Tinker's Cabin and then to the Butterfly Field. By estimating her measurements, she marked how far she believed they had traveled.

"Father's map doesn't mention Hermes' Wing. There is no Butterfly Field. But it seems the line continues much farther beyond the Tinker's Cabin and then ends. Given my calculations, we are nearing the end of his journey. It's almost as if there is a destination with no name. It could be Hermes' Wing."

She asked Sir Topas, "Do you think we are close?"

"As I've previously made plain, I'm not interested in this whole letter thing. I told you not to ask me anymore about it. I'm merely interested in getting home to where it's warm and dry."

"So, you like our dusty village?" Barjinder asked.

"In fact, I do! And the food is much better as well," Sir Topas retorted.

The breeze introduced a chill that Barjinder struggled to ignore. They pressed on. Barjinder sang songs to comfort herself. She was surprised when Sir Topas joined in. She knew then why Durga insisted she take the parrot with her. He was good company. She fed him seeds as reinforcement, and with each tidbit he sang more gloriously. Barjinder was growing quite fond of him.

"I've prided myself on my vocal cords. I'm quite talented, you know," he boasted.

"You are!" Barjinder affirmed in good-natured agreement.

"In addition to my singing capabilities, I am quite adept at using my beak. The delicate curvature allows me to do the most complicated of tasks. We are known in my family for delicate curvature, you know."

Barjinder had gotten used to his boastful confidence and found it endearing. "Really?!" She feigned interest as her mind wandered to the dread in her stomach. Could they really be nearing the end of the journey? The Tinker made too many warnings of danger to believe they were close to Hermes' Wing.

She spotted a rocky outcropping with the mountains proudly perched behind. As they approached, Barjinder realized the only path that would afford them to the land beyond would be down through the rocky field. Their path began to descend and Barjinder scrambled down, sometimes sliding on her backside, around the biggest boulders. The way passed straight down with only more dark rock in sight. The cold intensified.

Barjinder anticipated Sir Topas's comments, which came in a nervous string: "I do not like this path. I don't do well in the cold. Is this the right way? I do not believe this is the right way!"

"Sir Topas. We have committed to this path now. I cannot get you back up again without much distress."

"Surely you should have exercised better judgment! Next time listen to me. And follow my directions!"

Though Barjinder wanted to protest that he had never given her any directions, she was silenced by her own doubts. Perhaps he was right. This didn't seem like the right way. The air was cold around her face.

She tucked Sir Topas inside her sweater and perched him on her shoulder to protect him from the wind. He accepted the protection with gratitude.

Now, he talked from under her sweater. "You know, traveling while you can't see is really quite rewarding. It makes it easier to dream of enjoying tea time, gossiping with friends, and other luxuries I've left behind. Did I ever tell you about the full-cream scones with apricot and rosemary butter at my Aunt Martha's?"

The lower the pair descended down the rocky way, the colder it became. Barjinder found herself wanting to turn around, but given the pitch of the wet rock, it would be nearly impossible to crawl out. She could only move forward.

Barjinder began scaling the face of the last series of boulders. With her pack on her back and the bird on her shoulder, each step had to be carefully made. Ahead she could make out a dark patch that seemed it might be a broad road. She carefully shimmied down, managing the shifting weight of the bird. But the rope tied on her pack caught an edge of rock. When Barjinder twisted to release it, she lost her foothold and slid with speed. Sir Topas was wretched from her shoulder and fell to the front of her sweater. She instinctively wrapped an arm around him and used the other to brace her skid to the ledge below.

"Quit squeezing me so hard," he called from inside her sweater.

Barjinder raised her body and peered below. The dark patch was no way out. It was a deep gash in the bottom of the rocky ravine—an unhealed wound in the cold earth. The crevasse traveled as far as she could see on either side of her and measured about two body lengths across. A bitter, wet freeze emanated from the dark.

Barjinder leaned back and wobbled with fear. From under her sweater, Sir Topas's head appeared.

"Get us out of here!" he cried, and he began furiously flapping from inside her sweater. The motion pitched her body forward, and she struggled to right herself.

"Get me out of here, I say!" He continued to struggle in panic.

Barjinder gently pulled Sir Topas out by his head, and he flapped his way up and landed on a boulder next to her.

"I've told you, it is much too late to turn around now. We have to find a way to cross the crevasse." Going back was not possible now. And she wasn't ready to give up. She remembered her father's words: "Move forward."

She saw the unwound cord that hung from her pack. If she could get the cord secured to the other side of the crevasse, she believed she could test her weight and cross it.

Barjinder lashed one end of the rope to the boulder and tied a bulky knot at the other side. She began to throw the cord across the crevasse to catch between two rocks. Once it caught, she explained her plan to Sir Topas.

"You will travel in my pack, and I will shimmy us across the rope."

"You've got to be kidding," he said dryly.

"No. You won't be able to see and you will enjoy the dark. All that's left for me to do is to test if the cord can hold our weight," she explained.

But when she pulled with all her might, the cord snapped away.

"I think another plan is in order," Sir Topas said unhelpfully.

"It needs to be lashed on the other side. If only I could fly like the butterflies," Barjinder thought out loud. At once, she remembered how far and how strong Sir Topas flew that day—much longer than the width of the crevasse. He could certainly hold the cord in his beak and lash it on the other side.

Sir Topas saw the churning of her mind. "Oh no, no, no, no. Don't look at me!"

Her thoughts were agile. "But the delicate curvature of your beak! You yourself said you could do many things with it. All you would have to do is lash the cord on the other side."

Sir Topas hesitated for a moment but quickly found his protest: "But I can't fly. Everyone knows parrots can't fly!"

"I know you *can*. I saw you in the Butterfly Field. Sir Topas, it's our only hope to cross! I will perch you on my arm and fling you across. You will only need to fly a couple of feet. You can do it. You are a bird, you know!"

Appealing to his pride proved to be the deciding factor. "Well, I suppose my choices are limited," he said uncertainly. "And if I can't make it that far, I can just fly back."

"Absolutely." Barjinder agreed with confidence.

Sir Topas accepted her arm. She placed the cord firmly within his beak. "Now, fly as hard as you can and I'll yell directions to you once you're on the other side."

She swung her arm and the parrot flapped with conviction. Barjinder saw him rise and felt great relief. He was going to make it. Then suddenly, he stagnated in the air and she watched in horror as gravity pulled him down, plummeting into the depth of the crevasse below.

Barjinder screamed, "Sir Topas!" Fear replaced any ability to think as he disappeared from view. In the still darkness, she called to him desperately, "Sir Topas!" but heard no answer. She lurched for the cord, thankful to feel his weight on the end of it. She dragged his body up and pulled him to the rocky ledge.

Sir Topas lay on his side quivering, one wing twisted behind his back. Still, the cord remained firmly clenched in his beak. He had saved himself by hanging on.

"Oh, you're still alive!" she gasped, releasing his beak and taking out the cord.

"Yes," he managed to reply, "but hanging on by the skin of my teeth." He paused, his humor intact. "A metaphor, clearly."

"How badly does your wing hurt?"

"Well, I wouldn't say it hurts," he grimaced with an uncharacteristic squawk, "I'd say it's searing, completely mind-numbing pain!"

Barjinder tried to right the wing, but Sir Topas squawked more loudly, protesting the pain. She knew she must get him help. She secured Sir Topas as tightly as she could in her pack and gave him berth to breathe. Barjinder began traversing across the boulders on the shallow edge of the crevasse. She had to find another way. Her knees were rubbing raw as she scaled the edges of the slippery rock.

Sir Topas became strangely silent, and when she was able, she lifted her ear to the shallow puffs coming from his beak. "Why did I risk it?" she thought. "Why didn't I just turn around when I could? Is a letter worth all this?"

"Sir Topas?" she asked. "Talk to me."

She knew she loved her companion now. He was her responsibility. He must survive.

Sounds of water drew her to a small stream seeping into the crevasse from above. She decided to climb back up the dark slate of the rock. Each step took concentration and planning so as not to slide down. She forgot she was soaked, cold, and hungry as she climbed as hard and fast as she could. The water broadened and she crawled around the edges. At the top of the fall, she found a small tributary and waded through a creek bed.

Sir Topas had not made one sound the whole climb up.

THE RIVER OTTER

Sticks. Piles of sticks and debris stood directly in front of Barjinder, blocking the creek. She decided to go around the jam, and as she did so, the sides of her skull started to vibrate. She heard high-pitched noises—like voices from another world. The harder Barjinder listened, the more it hurt her ears. Then the vibrations stopped.

An otter slithered from the edge of the river. He looked straight at Barjinder and the vibrations began again, such that she could make out his tones.

"River flooding. Caution."

Barjinder remembered Sir Topas immediately and started excitedly. "I am in great need of help.

Finding Hermes' Letter

We have come out of the Great Crevasse. I have a beloved parrot that is injured. Please help us."

The otter seemed still, as if he couldn't understand her words. Was she speaking a language the otter could not comprehend? She heard the vibrations in her head and now in her body too. The otter sat up on his hind legs. He was trying to communicate with her. She faintly heard, "Animals help animals."

The otter approached her and the vibrations quickened. Barjinder heard, "Give me the bird." She protected her pack between her arms. How could she give him Sir Topas? Who was this animal? She whipped herself around and ran higher onto the riverbank. She looked behind. The otter did not follow.

Barjinder recovered her breath near a tall crooked tree. She sat and slid Sir Topas from her pack. The bird whined slightly, his wing now limp behind his back. His breathing was barely audible. Sir Topas was dying. What could she do?

Barjinder reached to the bottom of her pack and found the two pouches the Tinker had given her.

"One will heal you, the other will make you sick," he had warned. She had an equal chance of healing him. This seemed a risk she had to take. He had to be saved.

She found a sharp edge of stone, quickly picked a pouch, and lanced the tightly wound cord. She put her finger in and tasted the oily liquid. It was bitter.

She loosened Sir Topas's beak and drained the contents of the pouch down his gullet. He accepted it easily.

Barjinder's heart raced as she waited for the healing oil to work. Surely he would start flapping his wings. Or begin singing his songs. How she longed for his voice. A minute went by. Nothing. After two minutes his neck went limp. She put her ear to his feathery chest. His heart was slowing. She had chosen the wrong pouch.

She rushed to open the other pouch—this must be the healing oil. Perhaps if she used it now, she could reverse the other. She picked up the second pouch and then suddenly dropped it.

She had to hold her ears. A high-pitched vibration pierced her head and made it ache. A pod of otters raced toward her. Two advanced directly in front of her and separated themselves from the others.

Through the noise she recognized the words, "Give us the bird. He is ill and only we can help him now."

The screeching was so loud now, Barjinder could barely stand it. She looked at Sir Topas. But before she could respond, the second otter slid up, grabbed the bird, and rushed away. The rest of the family followed fast behind, leaving Barjinder alone with one small otter.

"No! Wait! Where are you taking him?" she cried. They moved much too quickly for her to chase. She sat down and hot tears shook from her body. She had endangered his life, and now he was lost to her.

The small otter curled next to her. His vibrations were slow and not as hard to hear. But her ears were still ringing from the band of otters, and she had trouble making out his communications.

"Come with me. I will help you cross the Great Crevasse," the young otter said calmly.

"What?" Barjinder had lost heart for the journey now. "I can't go on without Sir Topas. I need him."

"If my family can repair the bird, it will take many weeks. You do not have time to wait for him," he said calmly.

"How can I leave him?"

"You will travel alone now to search for your letter," the otter responded.

"This journey is not worth the letter. No, I must stay. I promised to return him."

"His life will be here with us. Animals help animals."

"But how can I continue?" Barjinder asked, her own heart aching with grief.

"You must not give yourself away. You must give your gifts away. Follow me." And the otter walked away.

Finding Hermes' Letter

Barjinder didn't understand his meaning, but she gathered her things and followed the otter. "What else can I do?" she thought. Her sadness at leaving Sir Topas was eclipsed only by the confusion she felt. Would she ever see Sir Topas again? If he could die in the Land of Nod, was her life in danger too? How could the search for her purpose be this hard?

They traveled back down the creek and onto the other side of the falls. From there, the otter scampered along a narrow pathway carved in the rock, and Barjinder struggled to stay close behind. Soon they came to a large pool of water.

The otter began. "There is only one way to cross the Great Crevasse, and that is to go underneath it—through the Deeps. This is a tunnel formed in the basement of time."

"But where is the entrance to the tunnel?"

"Here within the pool. The tunnel of the Deeps is filled with water. You must swim through the passageway to the other side. You must hold your breath and swim."

"How long is the underwater tunnel?" Barjinder asked.

"Great powers of concentration are needed to swim the distance. You have to be intently focused on your destination. You must fight fear and distraction. You will rely on your breath."

"But how long is the tunnel?" she asked again.

"It is different for each of us, but you will learn how to pass if you are dedicated to this journey."

Barjinder swallowed her need to cry. She didn't feel dedicated any longer. Her mind leaped toward figuring out the way back. How could she move forward now? She was a strong swimmer, but the water looked so cold. And the otter wasn't giving her the comfort she longed for. What if she didn't make it? And what if she did? She would leave behind Sir Topas forever.

THE DEEPS

The young otter didn't wait for Barjinder to decide. He began giving her detailed instructions to traverse the tunnel.

"Breathe deeply and dive toward the light. Do not fight against the water. Move boldly." Barjinder struggled to keep up with his words and remember what he was saying.

The otter motioned her to get into the water. Barjinder put her feet in the water and was surprised that it was not cold.

"Why is the water so warm?" she asked the otter.

"The water touches the hot rock at the depths of the earth," the otter replied. "Secure your pack so you may swim with it."

She filled her lungs with air and plunged into the water. It felt deliciously warm. She kicked underwater, opened her eyes, and saw a slit of light ahead. She popped up out of the water calling, "I see the light!" But the otter had vanished.

Barjinder was now completely alone. Fear sent her back down into the water to hurry to the other side. She followed the slit of light to the tunnel entrance but soon realized that she would not have enough breath to make it through. She returned to the rocky edge and pulled herself out.

She remembered the otter's admonishment to be focused. She decided that she must expand her lungs to take in more air. Slowly, she breathed in and out, in and out, filling her chest with as much air as it could hold. Then she filled her lungs broadly and dove with force from the edge toward the tunnel entrance.

Soon Barjinder was well within the tunnel. She kicked strongly while trying to conserve her energy. She felt she was making progress even though all she could see was light.

"What if I don't make it?" she thought. She told herself to concentrate, but fear flooded her. Her heart began to race. All she could see was light, and she was losing direction. "Will I drown here in the Deeps?" Her lungs burned. Her ears throbbed and her head was filled with the pressure of her beating heart.

Barjinder swam slowly now. Her limbs moved like a dancer in the water. The swimming was becoming easier and she felt she could breathe through the water. When she saw the light turn gold, she believed she was dying. A figure of a woman with a flowing gown showed itself to her. And as she moved to put her cheek next to hers, Barjinder's face burned. The woman floated beyond her with the golden light.

When Barjinder awoke, she was lying on her back with water lapping at her chest. When she rolled to her side, the sky spun and her head pulsed. "Sir Topas," she said. But there was no answer. She sat up on the gravel shore and rose to her knees. She headed out into the distance because she had to.

THE SYNAPSES

Barjinder wandered. Her head and heart were heavy from traversing the Deeps. There was no trail, no path now. The map was of no use to her. All she could see was an expanse of gray fields. She aimed for the highest hill in hopes of a vista to see her way. She didn't care about Hermes' Letter now. She only wanted to be home and become who she used to be. The sky spilled forth a deeper gray, and she felt lost in the space between earth and sky.

Deep rumbling just beyond gave way to flashing light. The lightning came in a spectrum of hues rushing toward her. She lay low to avoid the lightning crashing into her, and when she looked up she was surrounded in a net of electricity that seemed to radiate heat. Like the pathways in a brain, the field of flashing lights was a living, moving cloud of energy.

At each connection in the net, Barjinder noticed, small luminescent fairies appeared. They waved and moved, lighting more brightly when they spoke.

"Barjinder, the time is come for us to take you to Hermes' Wing."

"Who are you?" she asked.

"We are the Synapses. We are the field of power that lives within your imagination."

"Are you here to take me home?"

"We are here to help you find Hermes' Letter. We conform to your way of knowing. If you want to find the letter, you must create the destination in your mind and choose to pilot yourself toward it."

"That's what I've been trying to do here in the Land of Nod and I've failed."

"We will help you shape what you create in your mind. Try it. Imagine what you'd like to experience next."

Barjinder was exhausted and weakly conjured a picture of herself at home, but sadness overwhelmed her. "This isn't going to work," she said flatly.

Another fairy's connection lit up. "Rest with us awhile. Lie back on our net and let us hold you." The fairies flew together and bent their net of light energy behind her. It felt like the warmth of a fire. She scooted onto it. The power of the Synapses pulsed energy into her flesh.

The net began to fly up out of the cover of grayness, above the clouds and into the atmosphere. As Barjinder elevated, she felt hope. She began to imagine Hermes' Wing and the letter. She felt a swiftness of travel, as if the Synapses were responding to her direction. She started to imagine the details of what Hermes' Wing might look like and created thoughts of what she might find there. The fairies coalesced and thinned under her as if they were designing the contents of her mind.

Finding Hermes' Letter

As the Synapses flew her higher, Barjinder looked down and saw a structure built out of the side of a spiked mountain. The rounded walls of the building were formed from between the rock, and as she approached she could see they were made of glittering gold. The fairies' net began to descend gracefully. The flickering structure in the peak turned into what Barjinder recognized as the shape of a wing. This was the destination—Hermes' Wing. Great relief filled her. Now her journey would be fulfilled. The letter was near.

The net floated more closely to the earth, and she could see from above. Hermes' Wing was built as a labyrinth. Every part of the shape of the wing was a walkway lined in gold. There were others traveling to the pointed mountain, people scattered here and there on the approach. She saw that she had not been alone throughout the journey but closer than she realized to other travelers.

The Synapses settled her down to the earth at the base of the structure. The net placed her near the entrance to the maze. A fairy directed her, "Walk the labyrinth of the Wing and you will hear Hermes speak."

HERMES' WING

Barjinder lifted herself off the electric net. One of the Synapses flared, "You may walk only once into the labyrinth. When you have entered, you cannot turn back. You must go through completely if you are to receive Hermes' message. This is your time. Let no one go before you."

The Synapses wrapped themselves around her in an embrace. They enveloped her head, tightening their net around her hair. She felt their warmth and power being transferred to her as they flew away into the horizon.

She walked toward the entrance of the Wing. "I finally made it," she thought to herself. Her heart

Finding Hermes' Letter

was pounding, and she tried to calm down so she could pay full attention.

Barjinder heard a commotion from behind as a small band of travelers quickly drew near. She saw that one was carrying a limp body in his arms. It was clear this wanderer was in danger.

One from the crowd said, "Move away now! We found her at the edge of the Deeps. She will not live unless we rush her to Hermes for healing. She must go this instant."

Barjinder was confused. The fairy said it was her time to enter the labyrinth. She wanted to dart into the entrance but felt she must find a way to help.

Another in the crowd said, "You must sacrifice your hopes for the sake of another. This is the higher road. Surely this is more important than your asking Hermes for a letter."

Barjinder remembered the otter's words, "Don't give yourself away. Give your gifts away."

She quickly drew from her pack the pouch of healing oil she had received from the Tinker. She handed it to one in the group and said, "This will heal her." Barjinder turned quickly and ran toward the entrance to the labyrinth. Just before she entered, she turned to see the young girl raising her head.

Barjinder followed the gold walk and wound through the pathways ordered like feathers in a wing. As she walked, she waited for Hermes' voice and wondered how he would appear. Would a letter sail down from the sky? Would he appear in the air? She remembered all that she had been through and the advice she'd been given along the way. She remembered all she had lost and wondered what she would find. She only wished Sir Topas could have made it with her.

She looked up. She searched the edges of the labyrinth. With each turn in the walkway, no letter appeared. She considered going back and retracing her steps, thinking she might have missed it in passing or made a wrong turn. She listened intently for a voice. She slowed to a crawl to listen. She sped up. She yelled "Hermes!" But as she walked, no voice answered and no letter presented itself.

Finding Hermes' Letter

She turned the final corner of the maze and saw ahead the gold stone exit. Where had Hermes been? Where was her letter? Was the hardest journey of her young life going to end here?

Barjinder traveled to the exit and stood there refusing to step out. A wind blew from behind her as if it had traveled the walkway of the labyrinth. She said to herself, "Listen to the wind."

"Listen to the wind." But she wasn't exactly sure whether it was her own voice speaking or Hermes. "Listen to the wind." If she walked out of the labyrinth, she knew she would not find her letter. But she could not resist the voice in her head. She stepped past the last golden stone and followed the wind out of the Wing and into the open landscape.

THE WHISPERING WINDS

Barjinder now walked along on a raised knoll, the wind whipping from every side. She could see birds lofting on the high currents. The air was moving fast around her and she decided to lie on the earth and listen to the wind. Hours passed. But she could hear nothing.

Longing for her father and her home, she knew it was time to go. She had done her best. And she had failed. She had lost Sir Topas and her chance for her letter. Now she must turn away from the search for the letter and find her way home.

She wanted to leave the Land of Nod and be home at once. Night was falling. She knew she could travel by the light of the stars. She stood and saw streaked clouds ahead in the night sky, shielding the moon. While staring at the moon, there came through the clouds a kaleidoscope of light. The flashing of the heavens made the hillside look like a watercolor. She peered into the colorful sky. Here Barjinder saw the familiar woman with the flowing gown, her face filling in. She spoke to Barjinder the gentle words, "Do not try to find yourself. Create yourself."

The face was strangely familiar, though Barjinder couldn't make out her features. She only felt a vast shower of love engulf her, flowing around and through her.

Then with a start, Barjinder saw a sudden fanning of color appear at her side. She thought it was the light of the night sky, but then the fluttering took shape. From the spectrum of colors came the wing of Sir Topas, and then following, his full form. "Let's get out of here," he said. "You know how I hate the wind in my feathers." Barjinder's chest pressed for breath. She reached for him but then backed away.

"Forget me so soon? Just put me on your shoulder and let's get home!" he barked.

Barjinder reached to squeeze him to see if he was really alive. "Oh, Sir Topas!"

"Gentle now," he cautioned. "Follow the lights. They will guide us home."

Barjinder was thrilled to feel his feathers on her neck. Sir Topas was really back. She could return him now with pride.

They followed the flashes of color across the hillside and were guided to a tree at the border of the Land of Nod. There they slept beneath a low overhang of limbs until the rays of the morning sun woke them.

HOMECOMING

Barjinder and Sir Topas explained to each other all they had been through as they traveled out of the Land of Nod and back to the village. Barjinder described her swim through the Deeps, the Synapses' carpet of light, and Hermes' Wing. Sir Topas told of his dislike for the wet life of the otters and his general disdain for fish. "And besides, I was getting foot rot." Then he explained that the otters found a sound wave above time for him to fly across once his wing had fully healed.

"What do you mean a sound wave above time?" she asked in confusion.

"Surely you know time is created by the mind, for the mind. That's just elementary physics, my dear."

He explained with his characteristic superior air, yet she detected a tone of tenderness mixed with his words now.

"What do you mean?" she ventured again.

"Time does not bind me. My imagination allows me to move as I choose, when I choose. Of course, I've been to the Land of Nod many times. How do you think the Tinker knew your name? I told him you were coming." He laughed freely. "And you thought I wasn't capable of intelligent conversation!"

Barjinder remembered her words.

"Well, I hope you've learned something, my dear. Tell me I didn't break my wing for nothing!" he said. She didn't respond. He sensed her sadness.

"You didn't find your letter. Did you?"

"No," Barjinder said with resignation.

"A common casualty. You'll get over it."

Barjinder wasn't so sure. How would it be possible to give up the search for her unique purpose? As they turned and descended the hill out of the Land of Nod, she saw her small town and felt a pang of regret. She was going to miss the adventures she left behind. She wanted time to ponder all she learned. What did "create yourself" mean? And she needed time to share her feelings with Sir Topas.

"Sir Topas, you have been my greatest joy," she said softly.

He was quiet. "Sir Topas? Sir Topas! Talk to me!"

He stared straight ahead as if he didn't hear anything she said. "Sir Topas!" She realized she was losing him now as she traveled out of the Land of Nod.

Barjinder saw the townspeople starting to congregate when they spotted her hiking down the hill and back onto the plains. She heard raised voices from below. Rushing toward her was her father. They met just outside the thorny gate. His face was etched with relief. "Barjinder!"

"Oh, Father!" she cried as they embraced.

"My daughter. You are home at last!" He extended his grasp of her to look at her face. Barjinder's eyes were downcast.

"Father, I did not find my letter," she confessed.

He paused for a moment and then hugged Barjinder even tighter as if to comfort her. "Daughter."

"I tried, Father," she said, her voice muffled in his shoulder. She felt rest in his arms.

"All is well, Barjinder. All is well." Then he went on. "Did you find the rope I left for you, here at this gate? I hoped it would help you."

"Yes! I did find it! And I will tell you more, Father, when I am rested. There is much to say. But first I must return the bird." He released his embrace and let her go. She was greeted through the crowd, and all went to prepare a homecoming feast in the village square.

Barjinder headed to Durga's house with Sir Topas on her shoulder. Her feet shuffled in the brown dust. Home. She stopped to slip off her boots and feel the dust with her bare feet. She sighed, "How I'll miss you, Sir Topas. What will I do now?"

She heard him say in a low cackle, "You have been my greatest joy." She knew these mimicked words were his final blessing.

Barjinder continued toward the edge of town and rounded the back of Durga's house. She found Durga crouched low in the back garden. She didn't stand to greet her but continued grooming what seemed to be dead.

"So, you didn't find your letter," she said in a muffled tone.

"No," Barjinder admitted.

"Leave the bird on my shoulder." Durga stayed hunched low and busy.

Barjinder transferred Sir Topas to Durga's shoulder and gave him a rub under his beak.

"I see the henna still on your feet," Durga said abruptly. "Your mother drew the henna. Yet she longed for a canvas bigger than the human body." Barjinder was surprised to hear Durga mention her mother. She listened intently.

"Your mother found Hermes' Letter before you were born. Her purpose was to be an artist and see beauty in all things. You must have seen her paintings on the earth."

Barjinder knew her meaning. The woman with the face of light was her mother standing on the watercolored earth. Her mother was the one who had told her, "Create yourself."

Just as Barjinder began piecing the story together, Durga cut her off. "You may go now."

"But..."

"Take leave of me," Durga directed.

Recognizing the futility of asking Durga to share more, Barjinder touched Sir Topas once again and turned to leave. Her mind was racing, putting it all together. The vision in the steam at the Tinker's Cabin, the face whose light saved her in the Deeps, the woman in the colored sky who showed her Sir Topas and the way home – each was her mother. Her mother's spirit was guiding her from the beyond. And she was her mother's daughter. Just as her mother created her own art, so must Barjinder.

Here was the message she had worked so hard to receive. Her purpose was to create. She must create her own art, write her own letter, express her unique gifts in the world. She knew finding those best parts of herself would take time and courage, but her journey proved she was capable of much more than she thought possible. She would take risks and pursue her dreams of the city to the south, and more. As she walked home, Barjinder felt the full measure of her mother's love even without her presence. Joy and confidence swelled inside her.

Exhausted, she pushed open the paneled door to her house. She didn't shake the dust off her feet.

Finding Hermes' Letter

A certain lightness traveled with her. She surveyed her room and noticed everything the way she left it. Except one thing. On the desk there lay a letter. She reached for the envelope and held it for a moment before she sat down and opened it.

The sheet of paper contained a single sentence: "Write here your letter to the world. — Hermes."

Barjinder drew up her chair, pulled out a pencil from the drawer below, and began to write, "Just this side of the Land of Nod…"

The End

Annette Moser-Wellman is one of the world's leading experts on innovation. Her company, FireMark Inc., works with leaders of Fortune 500 firms to create market breakthroughs. She has taught thousands of business managers how to use her model for creative thinking and apply it to develop new products and services. Ms. Moser-Wellman's clients include Coca-Cola, Starbucks, Disney, Expedia, Microsoft, and many more.

Based on her research of creative genius in the arts and sciences, Ms. Moser-Wellman's book *The Five Faces of Genius: Creative Thinking Styles to Succeed at Work* (Viking/Penguin) demonstrates how business people can learn to invent from the greats of history. She developed a profiling tool to assist others in understanding their personal creative style and become innovators.

In addition to speaking to corporate and public audiences, Ms. Moser-Wellman consults with firms on bringing innovation to organizations.

She has conducted research on innovation and technology for Northwestern University's Media Management Center. She is a guest lecturer at the University of Chicago Booth School of Business. She produces papers, webinars, and blogs on the intersection of technology and media.

Ms. Moser-Wellman holds an MBA from the University of Chicago and a Master of Divinity degree from Princeton Theological Seminary. Her undergraduate degree was in art, and she has an abiding interest in the lives of creative individuals. She lives with her husband and two daughters in the Seattle area. Ms. Moser-Wellman's passion is to help others find their genius and use it to transform the world.

www.ingramcontent.com/pod-product-compliance
Lightning Source LLC
Chambersburg PA
CBHW032023040426
42448CB00006B/711